HENRI J.M. NOUWEN

From

resentment to

gratitude

SYNTHSIS SERIES

NIHIL OBSTAT:
Mark Hegener O.F.M.

IMPRIMATUR:
Msgr. Richard A. Rosemeyer, J.D.
Vicar General, Archdiocese of Chicago

"The Nihil Obstat and the Imprimatur are official declarations that a book or pamphlet is free of doctrinal or moral error. No implication is contained therein that those who have granted the Nihil Obstat and Imprimatur agree with the contents, opinions or statements expressed.

COPYRIGHT ©1974 HENRI J. M. NOUWEN
PRINTED IN U.S.A.

FROM RESENTMENT TO GRATITUDE

EDITORIAL PREFACE

THE AIM OF SYNTHESIS SERIES

As the growing edge of knowledge inceases its pace and widens the domain of man, new vistas strike us which are both exciting and frightening. Although the spreading light reveals more and more the marvels of our universe, still the bordering darkness of the unknown expands along with it.

Nowhere is the uncharted field of the universe of being more deeply felt today than in the area which concerns man himself. Here especially our growing knowledge deepens awareness of the vast unknown beyond our present range of vision.

We have begun to realize that the project of comprehending man is indeed gigantic. It is the conviction of all who seriously contemplate the problem that only a multi-disciplinary approach and synthesis will produce a true picture. We find emerging a cooperative effort by those engaged in any discipline which bears upon understanding man and promoting his well-being. The human sciences, the arts, philosophy, religion and all the helping arts reveal him in the several dimensions of his complex pattern of life.

SYNTHESIS SERIES is intended to introduce the reader to the experience of using the multi-disciplinary approach when attempting to understand himself and others. We believe this will lead to his perceiving and relating to the entire human family more effectively —that is, more in accord with rich depth and breadth of all those realities it contains. We hope this will help reduce the confusion caused by the over-simplified "answers" to problems of living which used to be offered by specialists in various fields.

Instead of the easy or quick answers we propose that each individual make steady serious effort to achieve a rich syntheses of concepts developed by many disciplines. This appears to be the only method that holds the promise of yielding the fundamental answer —the meaning his own existence is supposed to have—a meaning so often fretfully and falteringly sought by everyone whether he admits it or not. The promise and its realization in personal experience provide sufficient motive to undertake and sustain the search.

But beyond this, one can foresee benefits which transcend individual well-being. For personal growth of many individuals brings about a *social atmosphere* which stimulates still further development toward a more meaningful life on the part of each member of the group.

This interaction between an individual and others is apparent when we observe the opposite process of deterioration. Just as the most disruptive factor in society is the urest caused by failure of its members to find the meaning of life, so the reverse holds true, that society will benefit at all levels in proportion to the success people have in their quest for the meaning they believe their existence is supposed to have.

SYNTHESIS SERIES, we repeat, is intended to introduce the reader to the new multi-disciplinary method in carrying out the search for the meaning his life is to have when viewed in reference to the destiny of mankind.

PREFACE

A spiritual director is one who helps a fellow Christian to search his heart for the Holy Spirit who is leading him towards fullness of life. Part of the challenge of direction is the discernment of this elusive Spirit through the human prism of emotion, passion, history and desire.

Henri Nouwen has the unique gift of being able to peer through that prism to the very source of light and darkness. In this booklet to seminarians he touches that unreflective and often unseen zone of human behavior and tells us that the Spirit cannot get through as long as the seminarian or priest is blocked up by resentment.

This insight is very helpful to the director who is often tempted to be more sensitive to the external spiritual order he must maintain in the seminary than to the emotional disorder of the individuals who sit before him. Thanks to Fr. Nouwen, both director and directed can listen more accurately to the mixed music that comes "out of the depths." And together, by means of a spirit of gratitude, both can discover the lifegiving Spirit.

Fr. Damien Isabell O.F.M.
Editor,
Journal *of the Midwest Association of Spiritual Directors*

FOREWORD

What is taking place in contemporary American seminaries and why is it happening? These are questions that are being asked by those involved in seminary education, by other concerned men and women and certainly by many seminarians themselves. Henri J. M. Nouwen offers a suggestion towards identifying both a problem and a solution. He calls for a change of heart, a change of attitude. He presents a challenge for seminarians to face some basic issues: How to overcome negative feelings and to be free to respond to life by means of a positive, creative ministry — a eucharistic life. Unless this response is begun in the seminary, how can it be found in one's own priestly ministry. Therefore, the National Federation of Catholic Seminarians is pleased to take part in presenting this booklet. It is our hope that it will provoke a greater awareness among seminarians of their responsibility to take an active part in their education and in their preparation to become the kind of priestly ministers that this age demands.

>   DENNIS C. DAY
>   *President,*
>   *National Federation of Catholic Seminarians*

INTRODUCTION

Speaking to seminarians in 1973 is a very difficult task, because there is much pain in our contemporary seminaries. But there is also much hope for new life. Therefore, I have to speak about both the pain and the hope. I do this with great hesitancy because I do not want to hurt anyone. Yet it is impossible to speak realistically about healing when the wounds have not been identified.

Let me start with a painful personal memory. A few months ago I was asked to spend a few days with ten seminarians who had come together to prepare themselves for their ordination. I expected to find a group of vital, highly motivated men, full of excitement about their ordination and the ministry that would follow. I expected a warm welcome and a great eagerness to spend time together discussing the burning issues of the Christian ministry. I expected a sense of sharing, developed over the years, which now could easily lead to common prayer and celebration. I expected thankfulness towards the many gifts of mind and heart received in the past, and hopefulness towards the things to come.

But none of these expectations was realized. In fact, I met a group of tired men who were far from excited at the prospect of another talk. Instead of hospitality I experienced a certain hostility subtly expressed by a total lack of interest toward me and my concerns. I felt a strong resistance against a mandatory retreat in the house that long ago must have been full of men, but now seemed to be a sad expression of past glory. I sensed a great hesitancy to talk or to pray together and I could see very little real interest in God or in man. The past was discussed with scorn and the future with a vague fear. When the final liturgy came, there was little to celebrate. Even the guitars could not hide that.

I do not want to generalize and say that this is the seminary mood of today, but after visiting different seminaries I cannot avoid the impression that what I saw in this small group cannot be called simply an exception. The strange paralysis which charasterized the seminarians in the week before their ordination seems to be part of a much larger paralysis which causes a great amount of suffering to many men who have great ideals but small hopes to see them realized.

In this presentation I hope to come to a better understanding of this paralysis and indicate ways in which this paralysis can be healed through education.

When I think about the present situation of many seminarians I have the feeling that many have become victims of the passion of resentment. It is from this passion that they have to free themselves in order to come to a life of thanksgiving, which is a real eucharistic life. Based on this conviction I want to divide this presentation in two parts: 1) The seminary as a breeding place for resentment, 2) The seminary as the fertile ground for gratitude.

PART I

THE SEMINARY AS A BREEDING PLACE FOR RESENTMENT

Why have many seminarians become so paralyzed? What has made them so cynical about their theological education and so fearful about their future ministry? What causes their lack of creative communication or healing communion? What has often made their minds so dull and their hearts so weak? What has happened to many intelligent and idealistic men who were willing to leave their families for the Lord but who, after 6 or 12 years of education, have lost much of their zeal?

I find this very hard to explain. You can point to the great and often unexpected changes in the church, to the sudden drop in vocations, to the decreasing popularity of the priesthood, to theological apathy, to the crisis in the territorial parish, to the psychosexual conflicts of many men and women, to the lack of creative leadership, to the all-pervasive depression in the country and to many, many other phenomena. But why are so many men giving in to these pressures, why do they lose their vitality and enthusiasm (meaning "en theos" *in God*) and why do they sell their soul so cheaply to a world which they set out to convert?

Although there is no one answer to these questions. I would like to suggest here that many have become the victims of one of the most powerful but also well-hidden passions: resentment. If there is any passion that has harmed seminarians and their teachers, it is the passion of resentment. This calls for some careful explanation.

Passion is the frustration of the power to act, to be creative. Sometimes this frustration expresses itself in the form of undirected rage or spastic violence, but more often than not it finds its way in the murky constraining pathways of resentment. And although resentment is less frightening and less visible than the violent outburst of anger, it is no less destructive. It is very hard to identify resentment. Quite often resentment is so deeply hidden that it is not even noticed by the resentful people thmslves. It is indeed a silent passion, often very strong in the silent majority of those who cannot act but are no less angry than the rest. There are very few violent seminarians, but many are resentful. And J. Glenn Gray makes it clear how harmful this passion is when he writes:

"Resentment deteriorates character as surely as does rage, if more slowly. It makes us accomplices in destruction and enables us to deny participation in such destruction, even to ourselves." (*On Understanding Violence Philosophically.* New York: Harper Torchbooks, 1970, p. 20.)

Resentment is a clinging sentiment. It makes you hang on to something or someone you do not like. A resentful seminarian is the one who says:

I do not like this seminary at all, but I have to stay here in order to be ordained. I hate to go through this long dull process of so-called education which constrains me more than it sets me free, but there is no choice. I wish I could take my formation into my own hands, but if I do so I will never be a priest. The classes I am getting are irrelevant to my future ministry, but if I do not attend them I will never be a minister.

Resentment is the paralyzed complaint, the slow anger, the murky fear, the dragging suspicion. Resentment is the passion that makes you feel very angry and frustrated with the people and the institutions on which you have made yourself totally dependent without being able to do anything about it. It is the passion that makes you know that all your complaints will have a sympathetic ear but that nothing, or very little, will be done about it, and that you are just one more voice in the long row of complainers. I have the strong feeling that many seminarians are very unhappy people without realizing it. They are wasting a lot of their time brooding about the second rate quality of their classes, about the dullness of their professors, about the poor leadership of the bishops, about the moralism of the Pope, etc. And all the way through they experience an all-pervading feeling of impotence and powerlessness and a gnawing feeling that the next generation's complaints will probably be the same as theirs.

Resentment is the passion of those who feel caught in a bad bind. And often the bind of the seminarian is that leaving the seminary makes him feel just as guilty as staying. Leaving is frequently experienced as a lack of perseverance in the great ideal to follow Christ in His ministry, but staying is experienced many times as a slow integration into a system that asks for endless compromises and does not allow for the full development of the Christian ideal. This strange bind often makes seminarians very jealous of superiors, pastors and bishops who seem to have the power to change but seem reluctant to use it, and also of hippies, love-making students and creative artists who have more freedom but do not like seminarians or the church. So seminarians become that strange type of people who do not feel at home in the world nor in the church and who have become "exiled in the midst of the kingdom" (Camus). They often feel isolated, cut off and full of self-doubt. They often hold on to customs, rituals and life styles in which they do not believe themselves and they are very often angry with their own lack of happiness, realizing the paradox of being "the grumpy children of God."

Resentment is very destructive. It is a smouldering passion preventing us from asking forgiveness and creating space for God's liberating grace. It takes away our inner freedom to act and makes us cling to negative feelings as our only way to find an identity. We then become what we are against, lose the freedom to witness for anything or anyone and regress to the small satisfactions of unexpressed anger.

There are two main areas where the passion of resentment manifests its destructive power: the area of the mind and the area of the heart. Resentment harms our intellectual as well as our spiritual formation. Let us look at that a little closer.

1) RESENTMENT AND THE INTELLECTUAL LIFE

One of the greatest frustrations of seminarians is related to their academic work. There are many reasons why seminarians are dissatisfied, but if resentment pervades the mood of a school very little learning can take place, since learning happens to the degree that the student makes his own life experience the main source of his understanding. Certainly in theology, where the human condition is constantly under scrutiny, it is essential that the student offer his own living to himself and others for reflection. But this calls for an atmosphere of trust in which students and teachers can be vulnerable to each other. But a resentful student closes himself off, hardens his heart and makes it nearly impossible for the teacher to touch his inner self where real understanding can take place. A resentful student is always alert for new food to feed his negative feelings and, therefore, almost forces his teacher into a defensive stance. On the other hand, a resentful teacher, not trusting the motivation of his students, tends to negate instead of affirm their talents and will find himself in an exhausting and often endless battle. So students and teachers, called to form a fellowship of learning where new insights can be born out of the confession of not knowing, find themselves creating distance instead of closeness, blindness instead of vision. It is not infrequent that students who had very original intuitions and visions when they entered the seminary close up while there and leave opionated and close-minded.

2) Resentment and the Spiritual Life

Even more than the intellectual life, the spiritual life is harmed by resentment, because spiritual growth calls for an ongoing willingness to take off our defensive armor and to create inner space where the Spirit of God can live. It requires the courage to criticize our greedy self and to open our hands and expectations. Spiritual development means constant care for that purity of heart where we can listen to the voice of God who brings us into a deeper communication with our inner necessities, that is, our vocation. But when you listen to the many daily conversations among seminarians concerning their seminary and its teachers, and observe the students and their life styles, the parish and its ways of operating, the church and its hierarchy, you wonder how pure their hearts really are to receive the gifts of the Spirit. When we are full of resentments and keep clinging to our complaints as our only morbid way of self-affirmation, then there is no room for God to enter and to set us free. Resentment curtails the movements of God's Spirit and kills the kingdom within.

The seminary is the place where our hearts and minds should be formed so that we can be available to others as a source of healing and new life. Resentment is the great temptation into which we so easily fall today and which prevents us from growing in heart and mind. This might seem exaggerated and a bit facile, but when you look at life in many rectories in this country you will be frightfully surprised to see how many lives of priests are destroyed by a biting resentment. When seminarians think that everything will be better when they can finally leave the seminary and enter the parish, or any other ministry, they are blindfolding themselves.

Resentment does not stop with ordination. It does not take much to realize that many rectories are houses where sharing or praying together has become hardly possible. Many priests are torn apart by a guilty conscience which tells them that the Christian community, about which they talk so much, cannot be found in their own house, that the hospitality which they proclaim is not possible in their own life and that the friendship and love which they need so much has to be found far away from their own altar and pulpit. The same paralysis that is so visible in many seminaries is all too visible in the field. And just as seminarians many priests feel caught: when they leave the priesthood they feel guilty because of the commitment they made to the church and also angry because of the lack of education, which often becomes apparent when they apply for a secular job. But when they stay they realize that they never will be able to make the changes they desire and that they will never be really happy. When men, who have felt resentful over many, many years, finally receive power, that power has been pervaded with so much fear and anger that often a revengeful conservatism seems to be the only option left. Thus we see a vicious circle closing with little or no space left for the Spirit of God to enter and to make everything new.

I described resentment as the great temptation for the seminarians and the priests of today only to let you feel deeply our enormous need for redemption and new life. It has become clear how resentment makes us men of little faith, little hope and little charity. The men I met at the ordination retreat showed how destructive the passion of resentment can be. Instead of a place where their hearts and minds had become free for God's Spirit, it had been the breeding place for resentment and there are real reasons to fear for the creativity of their future ministry.

But once we have confessed our constant tendency to give in to resentment we can start asking ourselves if we can create space for forgiveness and allow God's grace to make us into new men. If this is possible we can slowly eradicate the spirit of resentment and become free to develop the liberating spirit of thanksgiving in which new life can be received. We now have to speak about the seminary as the fertile ground for a spirit of thanksgiving.

PART II

THE SEMINARY AS A FERTILE GROUND FOR GRATITUDE

How can we break through the chains of resentment? How can we free ourselves from a passion that paralyzes ourselves as well as our ministers? The passion of resentment has very deep roots in our broken condition. Adam resented the fact that he was not God while knowing that he could not live without Him. Seminarians and priests who have a great dseire to be close to God and to serve the people in His name are closer than anyone to Adam's temptation to resent that He is the Lord and they are not. Our authoritarianism is more than an expression of insecurity. It is also a reminder of our temptation to resent God for being God. Rebellions usually start in the palace of the king himself. And if we cannot sit on the throne we at least want to sit very close to it. If we do not dare to ask for it ourselves then our mother will ask for it. "Promise that these two sons of mine may sit one at your right hand and the other at your left in your kingdom" (Matt. 20:21). Maybe the expression: "If you can't beat it, join it," is the popular version of the dynamics of resentment which makes us spitefully look for the second best place in the kingdom when we are not able to conquer the first. Ministers who perceive themselves as those who had to be content with the second best place can only look upwards with resentment and downwards with suspicion. Then neither God nor man can be served.

Education to the priesthood has to be formation by which resentment can slowly be converted into gratitude. Real seminary education is to make rivals into friends, revengeful competitors into thankful receivers. This might sound pious but it really asks for the humble recognition that our life is not an inalienable property to be defended but a gift to be shared. All we have is given to us. The only thing we can give is thanks.

To give thanks, however, is no small thing. Since all that we are and all that we have is given to us, gratitude is the primary response to life. Gratitude moves us to handle everything that lives as a gift to be cared for, nourished and brought to fulfillment. It is significant that the central act of the Christian community is the "Eucharist" which means: "thanksgiving." There we open our hands and hearts to the Giver of all gifts and are reminded that life is not to be owned or possessed but to be shared and finally given away.

It is through this "Eucharistic" life that resentment can be overcome, and a new way of living becomes possible.

Resentment blocks action, gratitude allows it. Resentment makes us cling to our negative feelings and prevents us from moving forward. Gratitude opens us to new possibilities, new hopes and expectations. Resentment makes us prisoners of our own ambivalence. Gratitude helps us to transcend the bad binds and to follow our vocation. Resentment exhausts us by complicated jealousies and by draining desires for revenge. Gratitude takes our fatigue away and gives us new vitality. Resentment entangles us in the endless conspiracies of the world, often pulling us down to banal pre-occupations. Gratitude anchors our deepest self beyond this world and allows us to be involved without losing ourselves. Resentment finally takes and "mis-takes," gratitude gives and forgives. If any change is important in seminary education it is the change from resentment to gratitude. Many very concrete changes might be necessary. Maybe some seminaries might call for a total revision of their curriculum, for new staff, new libraries and new programs. Maybe some seminaries might need to take a very careful look at their training programs for future ministry and make plans for carefully supervised field work. Maybe more attention might be necessary for spiritual formation in which liturgy, spiritual guidance and instruction in mystical and ascetical theology can work together to help the students mature in the experience of God. May be more emphasis should be placed on ecumenical theology, the study of the Rabbinic tradition, or on the exploration of the message of Buddhism and Hinduism for the West. Maybe we might even need the courage to ask ourselves if our time does not ask for less Roman Catholic concentrations and more possibilities for seminarians from different churches to live, work and think together. Maybe we have to start wondering if the time of separate seminaries hasn't passed and maybe we are being challenged to look for totally new ways of theological education and spiritual formation whereby a creative interaction between different people, different disciplines and different religious traditions can take place. Maybe — maybe. But any change coming forth out of resentment is not worth it. Any change motivated by jealousy, revenge, bitterness or sheer frustration creates new ways which are just as old as the former, leaving the most destructive passion in the church untouched.

But once we can free ourselves from the passion of resentment and accept our life as the great gift of God asking for gratitude, then we can take the responsibility for our own education into our own hands and make decisions about how we study, where we study and for what we study, with a pure heart, obedient to the call of Him who wants to set us free.

Gratitude is the basis for a creative seminary education and a creative ministry because it makes us receivers instead of takers and allows us to see the pains and suffering of the world and the church, not just as disturbing interruptions, but as invitations for a change of heart. Not too long ago I met an old priest who said to me: "My whole life I have been complaining that my work was constantly interrupted until I discovered that my interruptions were my work." It is sad that he discovered this so late in life because resentment is exactly the complaint that life does not unfold the way I planned it to, that my many goals and projects are constantly interrupted by the events of the hour, the day and the year, that there is no other choice than to become the passive victim of the randomly-chained incidents and accidents of life. Conversion to gratitude means that I discover God as the God of history who is shaping and forming me day after day and who challenges me to be obedient, that is, to carefully listen to all that is going on and to wonder where God's hand is leading me. Then life is no longer a constant interruption of my little plans but the patient way by which God gives shape to His people, His world, and His church. Gratitude makes the interruption into an invitation and the moment of complaint into a moment of contemplation.

Here we touch the core of theological and spiritual formation. It is a formation of gratitude, that is, a growing receptivity toward God and His people. It is not a way to develop a technique to conquer God or to manipulate people, but a way to slowly create space where God can reveal Himself and where man in need can enter and ask for compassion. A resentful man can neither pray nor minister, but a grateful man can receive both God and man in the center of his heart. Gratitude is the core attitude out of which theological as well as spiritual formation can take place.

1) GRATITUDE AND THEOLOGICAL FORMATION

Theological formation is the gradual and often painful discovery of God's incomprehensibility. You can be competent in many things, but you cannot be competent in God. Theological education is a long process leading us to the humble confession that God is greater than our mind and that He cannot be caught within the limiting boundaries of our concepts. Good seminary education leads us not to a proud understanding but to an articulate not-knowing, a *docta ignorantia.* This is very hard to accept in a culture that suggests we are trained to master a subject, to control our destinies and rule the world. Doctors, lawyers, and psychologists study to become qualified professionals who know what to do and are paid for it. A well-trained minister can only prevent himself and others from narrowing God down to their own little expectations and to keep space open where God can reveal Himself. Ministry is the profession of fools and clowns telling everyone who has ears to hear and eyes to see that life is not a problem to be solved but a mystery to be entered into.

Last year I met a Methodist minister from South Africa who came to the U.S.A. for an extra year of training. He said:

"When I felt called to become a minister the Methodist Church sent me immediately to a parish where I preached and taught religion with much conviction and great success. I felt I knew who God was and what people had to do to be saved. But then after three years the Church sent me to the seminary." I asked him what he learned there. "Nothing really," he said. "I started to question myself, to doubt and to wonder how I could have been so sure about so many things. I read many commentaries on the Bible. I studied Barth, Bultmann, Rahner, and Schillebeeck. I heard about Kierkegaard, Sartre, Heidegger and Camus and I finally realized that I really didn't know who God or man was. But that growing ignorance made me gentle and understanding, and when I returned to the parish I at least could hear and listen to the painful search of my own parishioners."

The seminary education had emptied him out and made him receptive to the guest for meaning in many people's lives. Instead of clinging to his own small preconceptions, he slowly discovered that God was not just father or brother, love or justice, awesome or gentle, but that He becomes known to us by our constant confession of the limits of our human symbols. Yet this articulate confession of not-knowing created the space in which God could reveal Himself and where this minister could receive Him in gratitude.

2) Gratitude and Spiritual Formation

Even more than our mind, it is our heart which needs to become empty for the Spirit. This process of emptying is called spiritual formation. It is the preparation of the way, it is the gentle but persistent taking away of everything that can prevent the Spirit from entering. A resentful heart has no space for the Spirit. It is filled with worries, jealousies, revengeful thoughts and clings to its own suspicions as to valuable property. It takes much love and attention to slowly detach our hearts from their many occupations and preoccupations and to let the Spirit live in us. This is difficult for us who suffer from many uncertainties about ourselves, our present situation and our future direction. But these same uncertainties can also become our "Kairos," that is, our unique opportunity to unmask our illusions and to convert our fearful dreams and phantasies into the prayer of a contrite heart. Spiritual formation is the practicing of the paradox that prayer asks much effort but can only be received as a gift. The seminary is meant to be a school for prayer, a training ground for the encounter with God, but, at the same time, the place where we can wait quietly for Him who comes on His own initiative. Simone Weil rightly says: "Waiting patiently in expectation is the foundation of the Spiritual life." (Patience comes from *patior,* which means suffering, and it is only through this purifying suffering that our hearts can become ready to receive the Lord in gratitude).

Just as theology asks us to detach our mind

from the temptation to comprehend God, spirituality asks us to detach our heart from our inclination to capture God in any special emotion. God can never be identified with a good, warm feeling towards our neighbor, nor with the sweetness of our heart, nor with ecstasies, speaking in tongues, movements of the body or handling of snakes. God is not just our inclinations, our fervor, our generosity, or our love. All these experiences may remind us of God's presence, but their absence does not prove God's absence. God is not only greater than our mind, he is also greater than our heart. And, just as we have to avoid the temptation to adapt God to our small concepts, we also have to avoid adapting him to our small feelings.

When we are really spiritual men, when we have thrown out our resentment and created space for God's spirit, then we can be really creative men. We can then be critical and make decisions motivated not by fear, but by a deep desire to be faithful to God's call, and to follow Him whereever He wants us to go, even if that is outside of the seminary. It has never been revcaled to us that the seminary is the only or the best way to follow Christ, but it has become clear that to follow Christ means, primarily, to live your life just as authentically as He lived his, and every compromise in this authenticity is the road back to resentment.

Theophan the Recluse, the Russian Orthodox monk of the 19th century says, "To pray is to stand in the presence of God with your mind in your heart." When our mind has become full of the Lord and when we have emptied our heart, then we can descend with our mind into our heart and stand in the presence of God, realizing that all we have is given to us and that the only thing we can give is thanks.

So theological and spiritual formation, the two main aspects of the seminary vocation, require an articulate not-knowing and a receptive emptiness through which God can reveal Himself to us. As long as we think about seminary education as the way to the power of a profession, we forget that if ministry has anything to profess, it is poverty of mind and heart. Seminary education is not an education to power but to a creative weakness in which God's strength can manifest itself. It is in this weakness that we can receive the life of the Spirit in gratitude, and become the way without being in the way.

Maybe we should think about ourselves as a strong rock wall, resisting anyone who tries to enter into it. Real formation to the ministry is to allow God to carve His way into our rock and pull out the many stones of resentment. Everytime a stone rolls out of our wall, small or large, it hurts. Everytime we have to give up a familiar and seemingly safe concept, idea, plan or lifestyle we feel an inner protest. But when we are willing to see God's hand at work, we might discover that after much carving we have an empty cave where many lonely people can take refuge and find healing. Resentment makes us blind to God's carving hand but gratitude makes us recognize that slowly, but definitely, we are being prepared to be men who can offer our own pains as a source of healing for others.

CONCLUSION

I started this presentation with the sad story of a resentful retreat. In that retreat the liturgy could hardly be a celebration because resentment cannot be celebrated. I tried to show how destructive the passion of resentment can be, not only in the life of the seminarian, but also in the life of the priest. And although many charges, even very radical changes, may be necessary in the formation of future priests, essential for all changes is the conversion from resentment to gratitude. The preparation for the priesthood should be a preparation to a life of gratitude, a life of thanksgiving, a eucharistic life.

Seminary education in the final analysis, is education to the eucharist, not as an isolated event in every day or week, but as an expression of an understanding of life as a gift of God in Jesus Christ inviting us to unending gratitude. Once we enter this eucharistic life we can let our resentments go and stretch out our arms to Him who sets us free, free to take responsibility for our own life and ongoing education, free to be obedient to the Spirit in us, free finally to serve the people, not as a heavy obligation, but as a manifestation of our gratitude. In that freedom we take bread and wine and celebrate the presence of the Son of God in our midst until he comes again.

EXISTENTIALISM AND ITS IMPLICATIONS FOR COUNSELING .... .65
M. Emmanuel Fontes

A study in depth which leads to seven general principles for integrating existential insights into counseling.

THE CREATION OF FULL HUMAN PERSONALITY .... .65
Joseph Drew & William Hague

Complete psychological growth is a process inseparable from total reality—biological and spiritual, internal and external. Vocation is important.

SEX AND EXISTENCE .... .65
Adrian van Kaam

This booklet describes psychological, social and religious factors which hinder or promote the integration of sex and human existence.

NEW EDUCATIONAL METHODS FOR INCREASING RELIGIOUS EFFECTIVENESS .... .65
Dean C. Dauw

Special group methods of self-education that have proved helpful to others are also helpful to religious organizations.

LOVE AND SELFISHNESS .... .65
Alice von Hildebrand

True love cannot be separated from a joyful readiness to make enduring sacrifices for the sake of the beloved.

PERSONAL IDENTITY AND RELIGIOUS COMMITMENT .... .65
Francis Forde

Religious commitment calls for a mature judgement and consistent fidelity and creative care.

NEW LOOK CELIBACY .... .65
Rosemary Haughton

A vocation to celibacy is a sign of the Christian orientation toward the eternal life. This booklet reveals its larger dimension.

A PSYCHOLOGY OF THE CATHOLIC INTELLECTUAL .65
Adrian van Kaam

The split between secular and religious learning rooted in psychological history must be healed to prevent disaster.

EMOTIONAL DEVELOPMENT AND SPIRITUAL GROWTH .65
Timothy J. Gannon

To what extent can insights into a man's emotional life contribute to the solution of problems of spiritual growth.

LITURGY IN ADOLESCENT PERSONALITY GROWTH .65
Marygrace McCullough

The Liturgy does contain personality building forces that can be used effectively on the adolescent level.

PSYCHOLOGICAL DEVELOPMENT AND THE CONCEPT OF MORTAL SIN .65
Robert O'Neil & Michael Donovan

This booklet challenges the premise of current sacramental and educational practice that children can be guilty of mortal sin at the age of seven.

THE ADDICTIVE PERSONALITY .65
Adrian van Kaam

A psychological study of the origin, structure and function of the personality prone to addiction.

SPIRITUALITY THROUGH THE AGES .65

Our understanding of God and his love has shifting emphases. The contour and quality of our response will vary from time to time.

A PSYCHOLOGY OF FALLING AWAY FROM THE FAITH .65
Adrian van Kaam

A rare insight into this problem by a theologian with a psychologically oriented background.

UNDERSTANDING AND ACCEPTING OURSELVES AND OTHERS .... .65
William Zeller

Self-knowledge is important for mental health. Healthful growth of the individual depends on social development.

WHAT'S WRONG WITH GOD .... .65
Thomas M. Steeman

A probing search into a question that has practical ramifications for the modern man.

HELPING THE DISTURBED RELIGIOUS .... .65
E. F. Doherty

Like everybody else religious have problems of tensions and anxieties. Their causes and manner of handling are treated with sensitive insight.

WORLD POVERTY . . . CAN IT BE SOLVED? .... .65
Barbara Ward

In depth analysis of the problem of world poverty with sensible suggestions on how to solve it.

THE PRIESTHOOD: MASCULINE AND CELIBATE .... .65
Conrad W. Baars, M.D.

Psychiatrist, author, and consultant on the problems of the priesthood at the 1971 Vatican Synod of Bishops, Dr. Baars develops the positive values of celibacy and a regimen to achieve a priesthood both celibate and masculine.

THE RIDDLE OF GENESIS .... .65
Robert Koch

The study of comparative religion and modern biblical exegesis help to convey the essential message of the first eleven chapters of Genesis.

THE CHURCH TODAY .... .65

Important studies by men like Ratzinger, Schweizer, Congar, Pauwels and Winkhofer on various aspects of the Church in the modern world.

GROWTH TO MATURITY .... .65
Peter Cantwell O.F.M.

Maturity is not an accident of living. It is an achievement whose roots reach back to the very beginning of life, and are nurtured in successive stages.

THE DEFINITION OF THE CHRISTIAN LAYMAN .... .65
Edward Schillebeeckx O.P.

This author has established his right to speak with authority on a subject that is very important today. He bases his observations of Vatican II documents.

THE QUESTION OF FAITH IN THE RESURRECTION OF JESUS .... .65
Leonardo Boff O.F.M.

There have been many new interpretations of the Resurrection of Christ. These are investigated and contrasted with traditional belief.

HOW TO TREAT AND PREVENT THE CRISIS IN THE PRIESTHOOD .... .65
Conrad Baars, M.D.

A well-known psychiatrist, from vast experiences, discusses the role of the Church in the causation, treatment and prevention of the crisis in the priesthood.

FROM RESENTMENT TO GRATITUDE .... .65
Henri J. M. Nouwen

Challenges seminaries to overcome negative feelings and respond to life by a positive creative ministry.

THE MESSAGE OF CHRIST AND THE COUNSELOR $1.95
John Quesnel

An expert discusses the principles of counseling in general and pastoral counseling in particular as gleaned from the life of Christ.

Synthesis Series is published by
FRANCISCAN HERALD PRESS
1434 WEST 51st STREET
CHICAGO, ILLINOIS 60609